Other books produced by Colin and Eithne N...

The *Picturing Scotland* Series: a book for every part of Scotlan...

Aberdeen
Aberdeenshire
Argyll
The Isle of Arran
Arran & Ayrshire
The Borders
*The Cairngorms**
Caithness & Sutherland
Caledonia
Coll & Tiree
*Distinguished Distilleries**
Dumfries & Galloway
Dundee
Dundee & Angus
Edinburgh
Fife, Kinross & Clackmannan
Glasgow
Inverness
Islay, Jura, Colonsay & Oronsay
Lanarkshire

Lochaber
Loch Lomond, Cowal & Bute
Loch Ness
The Lothians
*Moray-Speyside**
Mull & Iona
Orkney
Orkney in Wartime
The Outer Hebrides
The City of Perth
Highland Perthshire
Ross & Cromarty
Royal Deeside
Sacred Scotland
Scotland's Mountains
Scotland's Wildlife
Shetland
The Isle of Skye
Stirling & The Trossachs
The West Highland Way

Commissioned Books (*In-Camera* format)

The Cairngorm Reindeer Herd

On a Rising Tide by Charlie Phillips
A photographic celebration of Britain's largest Bottlenose dolphins
Large format: 10" x 10"

ELGIN

AN *IN-CAMERA* BOOK

Colin Nutt
Author and photographer

NESS PUBLISHING

2 Elgin's Cooper Park is one of the town's great amenities, not least because it frequently provides onlookers with sights like this beautiful sunrise. At the time of writing, an otter has become a regular

ELGIN

visitor to the park's pond . . . see next page.

Welcome to Elgin!

Delving into the history of Elgin has been both a challenge and a joy. There's such a lot of history to discover! For instance, it has been home to our ancestors for millennia. Confirmation of this was discovered in 2002 when building developments in the north of the town unearthed pots, urns and arrowheads dating from at least 5,000 years ago. Later on, from roughly the 2nd to 10th centuries, the Picts left more substantial evidence of their culture, mostly in the form of intricately carved stones. An excellent example stands in Elgin Cathedral churchyard (see pages 6 & 69).

Where does the name of 'Elgin' come from? It seems unclear. Norse mythology refers to a character called 'Helgi'. There are records of a Norse earl of that name, born about 855, who reputedly ruled the Hebrides from his Orkney powerbase. Given Norse influence over much of northern Scotland in those times, it is conceivable that Elgin is derived from Helgi. However, it *might* have come from the Gaelic source 'Eilginn', said to mean 'little Ireland'.

There were two main causes for the growth of Elgin. The first was the castle, located atop Ladyhill at the west end of town. The second was the Cathedral, begun around 1224, at the east end. The stimulus of these two powerful influences led over time to the town filling in the space between them. There seems to be no precise date for the founding of a fort on Ladyhill. It would originally have

A winter night's view from Elgin Castle looking east across the town, with St Giles' Church prominent. The bench is the Elgin Burns' Seat which commemorates Robert Burns' visit to Elgin in 1787.

been a timber construction and must have been built before 1040, as the mortally wounded King Duncan was taken to the stronghold after a battle with Macbeth, Earl of Moray, that took place at Pitgaveny, north of Elgin. Following Duncan's death, Macbeth ruled Scotland until 1057.

    Moving on a century, in 1130 King David I took control of Moray and built a stone castle to replace the wooden fort. From this impressive base he solidified his grip on the area. Royal Castles were good for the local economy and ordinary people set up homes at the foot of the hill for the protection it offered. Such proximity was also convenient for local merchants supplying the castle's needs. The town must have grown in that period, for in 1136 it was Chartered as a Royal Burgh by David I. Many ups and downs followed through the ensuing centuries, bringing us to the Elgin of today. The county town's population of over 23,000 (and rising) is almost a quarter of Moray's total of 95,520 (in 2018).

6   The Pictish Cross which stands in the Cathedral grounds. Its main feature is the carved cross. Less clear are the carved portraits of the four evangelists which flank the cross.

Elgin is known for many things, but it's hard not to rate the cathedral as its best-known structure and greatest historic asset. Elgin Cathedral was the third largest in Scotland after St Andrews and Glasgow. Known as the 'Lantern of the North', its light was both physically visible for miles across the surrounding plain and spiritually enlightening for centuries. After the appalling attack by Alexander Stewart, the so-called Wolf of Badenoch in 1390, Bishop Bur appealed to King Robert III (the Wolf's older brother) for reparations saying 'My church was the ornament of the realm, the glory of the kingdom, the delight of foreigners and stranger guests: an object of praise in foreign lands'. Today, a visit to the cathedral repays as much time as one cares or is able to give it. It is a key component of Elgin's recently established and excellent tourist trail, 'Castle to Cathedral to Cashmere'. Elgin's motto, 'Sic itur ad astra' means 'This is the way to the stars' (see p.1). Enjoy our 'heavenly' city!

This stone on East Road marks the former 'Order (or 'Ordeal') Pot', a pond which once existed nearby. The name relates to how it was used to try suspected witches by the ordeal of ducking.

8   These thick stone walls are all that's left of Elgin Castle, a building that might have originally been three storeys tall. The castle's downfall began during Scotland's Wars of Independence, from 1296.

Today the Maryhill site provides good views over the town, in this case looking north-east over Borough Briggs towards the residential areas of Bishopmill and Lesmurdie.

10 While at the west end of Elgin, a fine May morning is a good time to take in the imposing sight of the original part of Dr Gray's Hospital, founded by Dr Alexander Gray in 1819.

This book works its way through Elgin from west to east, finishing at Johnston's of Elgin at Newmill. The picture gives a foretaste of further images of this world-famous brand's home on pages 78-79.

12 Tucked away on Elgin's western edge by the River Lossie, Glen Moray Distillery has been producing fine single malt whisky since 1897. Glen Moray is available in a range of expressions that will appeal to new

malt drinkers as well as connoisseurs looking for something a bit more special. The Visitor Centre welcomes increasing numbers of visitors who come for distillery tours and tastings. Above: the Still House.

14 After the First World War, a local MP funded the laying out of this garden and the building of these two cottages for war veterans. They are located at the west end of the town centre beneath Ladyhill.

At the top of Ladyhill stands the 24m/80ft memorial to the fifth Duke of Gordon. The column was erected in 1839, with the statue of the Duke (by Elgin sculptor Thomas Goodwillie) added in 1855.

16   On the south side of the town, Moray Street features a variety of architecture, such as this neo-classical building which houses Moray School of Art, part of Moray College, itself a part of the University of the

Highlands and Islands. Above: the new extension to Moray College, opened in 2015. It was established in 1971 as Elgin Technical College and today around 6,000 students are enrolled.

18 Still on Moray Street, this 'finial' was made by college students. It stands across the road from where Elgin's former Town Hall stood until it burnt down in 1939. On the right is the 1890 Victoria School of

Science and Art. Now looking in the reverse direction from the picture opposite, trees in the grounds of Moray College neatly frame the former South Church. At the time of writing it awaits a new owner.

20 The Inverness – Aberdeen railway passes through south Elgin. Occasionally, special trains traverse the route, such as this steam-hauled tour that appeared not so long ago. Elgin once had two stations,

the more grandiose of which was the Great North of Scotland Railway Station, opened in 1901. Although long closed, the building remains in use as a business centre. The old booking hall is pictured.

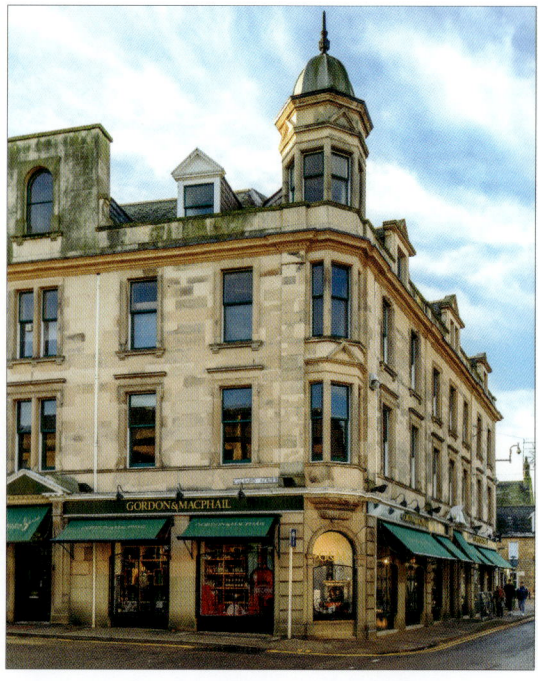

22 Left: now it's time to examine the town centre, starting at its west end where David Annand's *Wolf of Badenoch* sculpture stands. Right: on South Street, this is Gordon & MacPhail's fine emporium.

Virtually opposite, pedestrian-friendly Thunderton Place's attractive buildings offer a number of food and drink venues. The street takes its name from Thunderton House, one of Elgin's most . . .

24   . . . historic buildings, with its roots in the 11th century. Once known as the King's House due to it being a royal residence after Elgin Castle fell into disuse, it is currently undergoing restoration.

The heart of Elgin is the Plainstones, set out in 1787 for use as a market and 'feeing' fair (hiring of farm workers). Its oval shape adds a certain elegance to the layout of the town centre (quirky angles . . .

25

26   . . . notwithstanding!). The three-tier fountain, constructed in 1846, stands on the site of the medieval tolbooth. This was used for collecting taxes and as a prison. A later version also included council rooms.

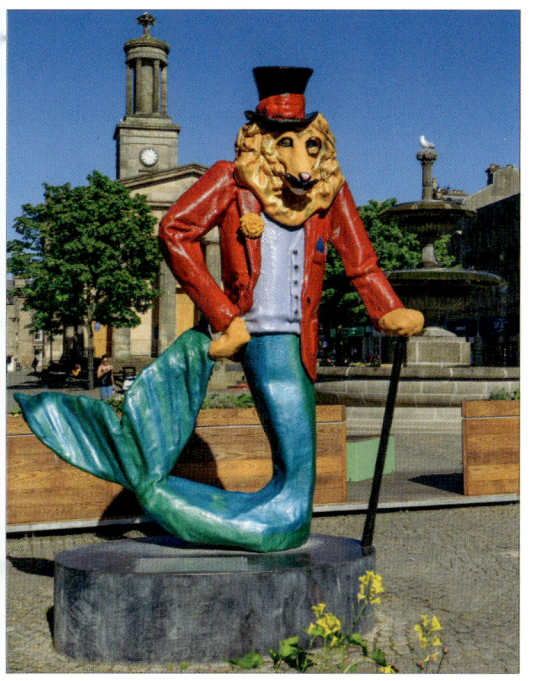

Left: many 'colourful' adjectives – as colourful as the Dandy Lion himself – have been applied to this statue at the Plainstones, unveiled in 2016. Right: close-up of the tower of St Giles' Church.

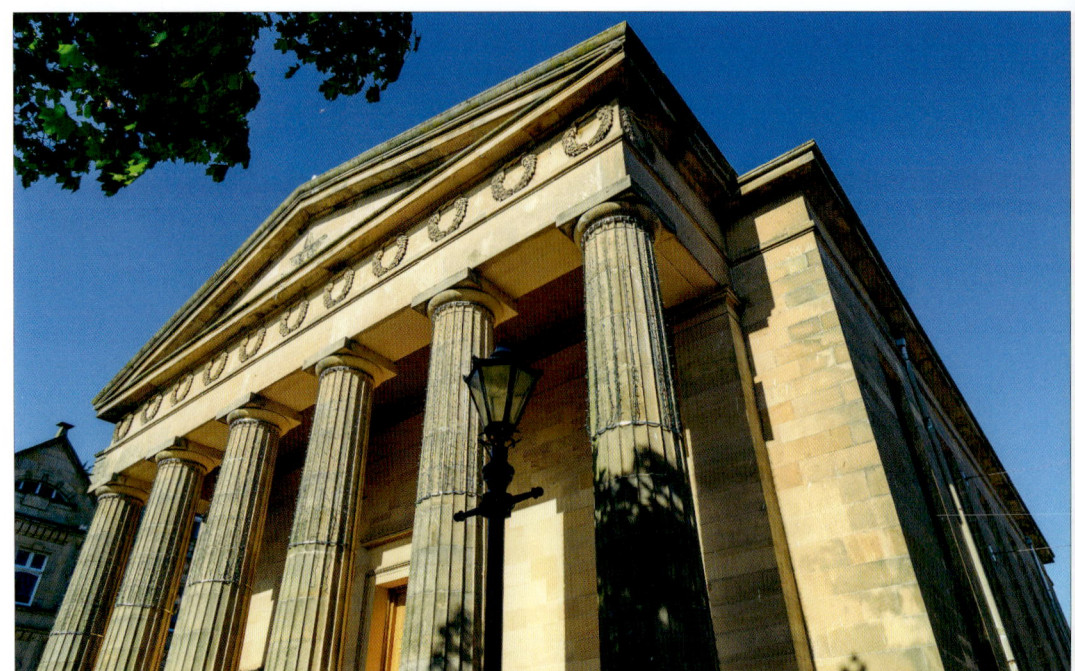

28 Replacing an earlier church, St Giles', designed by Aberdeen architect Archibald Simpson in the manner of a Greek Temple, with an imposing portico of six fluted columns at its west end, was built 1827-1828.

St Giles' tower rises to 34m/112ft. The upper section is a copy of the Choragic Monument of Lysicrates in Athens. The interior has a panelled gallery to three sides with a Greek key-patterned parapet.

30 Left: the War Memorial commemorates the 461 men of Elgin who died in the First World War. Right: further east along the Plainstones, The Tower (centre) is one of Elgin's oldest buildings, part of a house

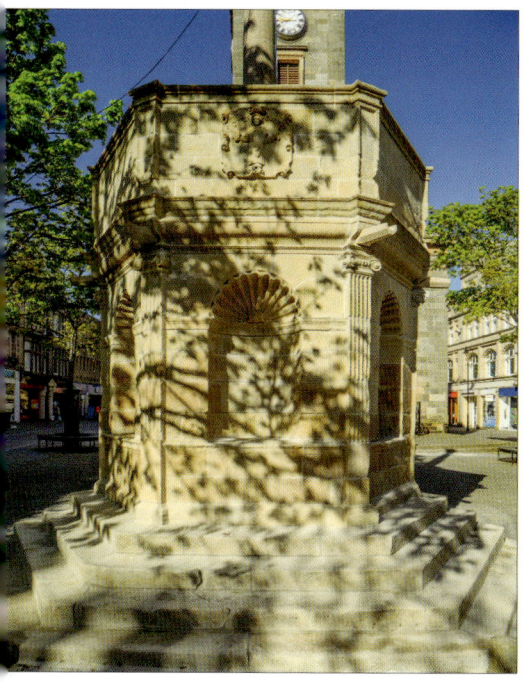

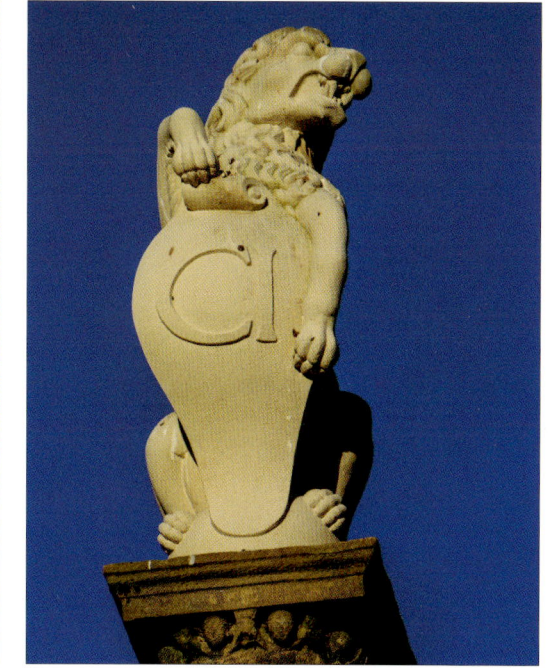

built 1634. Left: Elgin has had a series of market crosses down the centuries. This one – the Muckle Cross – was erected in 1888 and restored in 2017. Right: the new rampant lion carving atop the cross's column.

31

32 The Muckle Cross houses equipment that projects images onto the east end of St Giles' Church. At the time of writing, this giant slideshow features Elgin through the years, including some of its

olourful characters such as Peter Porridge Laing, the Elgin centenarian who lived to 103 (opposite).
bove: James Murdoch (b.1806), a.k.a. 'Cutler Jamie', a local labourer, metal worker and poet.

34 These two likely lads were, left: John 'Pickie' Gow, born 1846 in Elgin and chiefly known as a poacher; and right, James 'Punchie' Grant, b.1794, popular for giving away many of the fish he caught!

In what looks like a hand-tinted photograph, these ladies were involved in YWCA welfare work for munitions workers in 1917. Such projections are intended to be an ongoing feature.

35

36 Left: a Christmas view of the Muckle Cross and the east end of St Giles' Church. Right: the Town Drummer sculpture by Alan Herriot recalls how the people of Elgin were woken up – at 4am and 5am!

A house called Old Lodge was built in 1800 at North Port. It had extensive gardens in which there stood an ancient ornamental wall: all that remains is this archway, surmounted by a lion.

38 Elgin is a town of Closes. These narrow lanes and passages branch off at 90° to the High Street and were where much of the population lived. This one is Shepherds' Close towards the east end of the

High Street. The view above is from the opposite end and gives an idea of the limited space they offered. Life in the Closes was far from comfortable and generally quite insanitary.

40 At the east end of the High Street, on the left is the well-preserved townhouse built in 1694 which later became Braco's banking house. Through the entry (pend) to its right is the way to one of

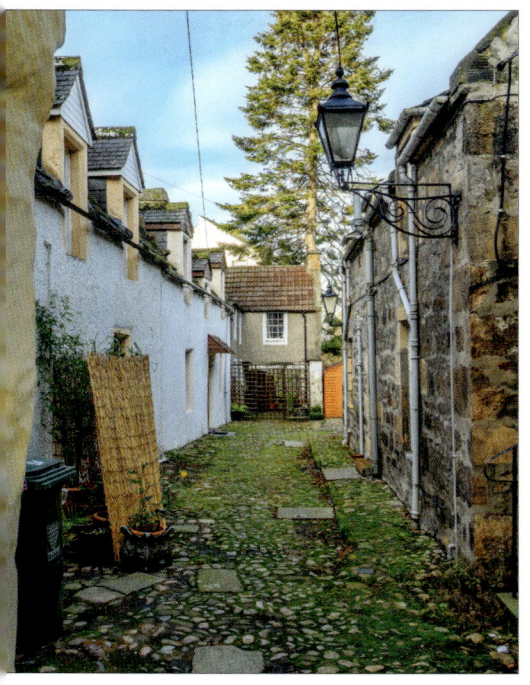

Elgin's more attractive closes, Braco's Close. Right: the Little Cross marked the boundary between the town and the cathedral sanctuary and became a place for public punishments.

42 Across the road is Elgin Museum, built in Italianate style in 1843, initially to provide a home for the numerous fossils discovered in local quarries. Today its exhibits are far more eclectic.

Moray Motor Museum has a superb collection of veteran, vintage, classic cars and motorbikes. Clockwise from top left: 1904 Speedwell; 1929 Rolls Royce Phantom 1; Bristol 403 (1950s); E-Type Jaguar (1960s).

44 Greyfriars Convent and Church on Abbey Street was founded in 1479 and rebuilt in 1896. This is its
    cloister. It remains a working convent run by a community of four Dominican Sisters. Its church contains

much of interest: the picture above looks from the altar towards the magnificently carved timber screen, through which the other half of the church can be glimpsed. Visits can be made by appointment.

45

46 Philanthropist General Andrew Anderson left a large sum of money to the town which funded the Anderson Institute. The building's roof sculpture depicts him with children of the poor he aimed to help.

Grant Lodge, built 1766-1790 for Sir James Grant, stands in Cooper Park. One of Elgin's great houses, at the time of writing it awaits restoration and a new role in the life of the town.

48 In 1899 Grant Lodge was sold to Sir George Cooper, an Elgin Lawyer. In 1903 he gifted the house and its grounds to the town, thus creating Cooper Park, a place of wonder on evenings like this . . .

. . . and days like this. The pond and the surrounding trees provide endless possibilities for photographers – or anyone who simply has the time to stand and stare. It also caters for those seeking recreation . . .

50   . . . by more active means, such as an informal game of cricket. The library stands beyond the grass, nowadays attached to the old Drill Hall (visible through trees on right). This was built in 1906 for

the Volunteer Battalion of the Seaforth Highlanders. Cooper Park cameos: above left: summer evening at the skate park; lower left: family of swans on the pond; right: evening light on one of the park's trees.

52 Cooper Park is extensive, giving a walk of about a mile around its perimeter. Its eastern part leads to the cathedral via this path where, in April, daffodils and flowering cherries bloom simultaneously.

Afterglow on a winter evening. The moon's fractured reflection sits in the pond. Cooper Park keeps on giving! It also provides a venue for outdoor events, a notable example of which was the Wolf of . . .

54   . . . Badenoch Re-enactment Weekend. This also featured sideshows and demonstrations, such as this spectacular and daring display on horseback. It got a lot more serious once the Wolf and his band of

'wyld wykkyd Helandmen' arrived. Real name Alexander Stewart, Earl of Buchan, he came to Elgin seeking revenge against Bishop Bur for ex-communicating him in 1388. There was bloodshed.

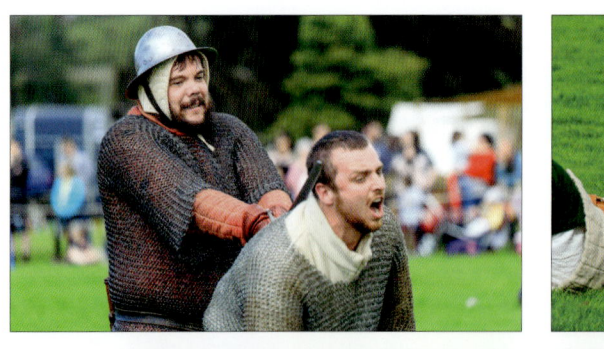

56 Clockwise from top left: he who lives by the sword . . . will die by the sword. Hawks were used for hunting and sport in medieval times . . . as were dogs like this wolfhound.

Left: Bishop Bur seems unimpressed by the pleas for mercy from this accused woman – his attention is elsewhere. Right: a tense 'parlez' between the Wolf and the bishop does not end well . . .

58   . . . and the cathedral was sacked and burned, as were 18 residences of the canons and chaplains and other buildings in the town. This montage image is another of those projected on St Giles' Church.

The extent of the cathedral remains today correspond to the expansion it underwent from 1270 following a fire. The west towers do not seem to be part of the original design but belong to the first phase.

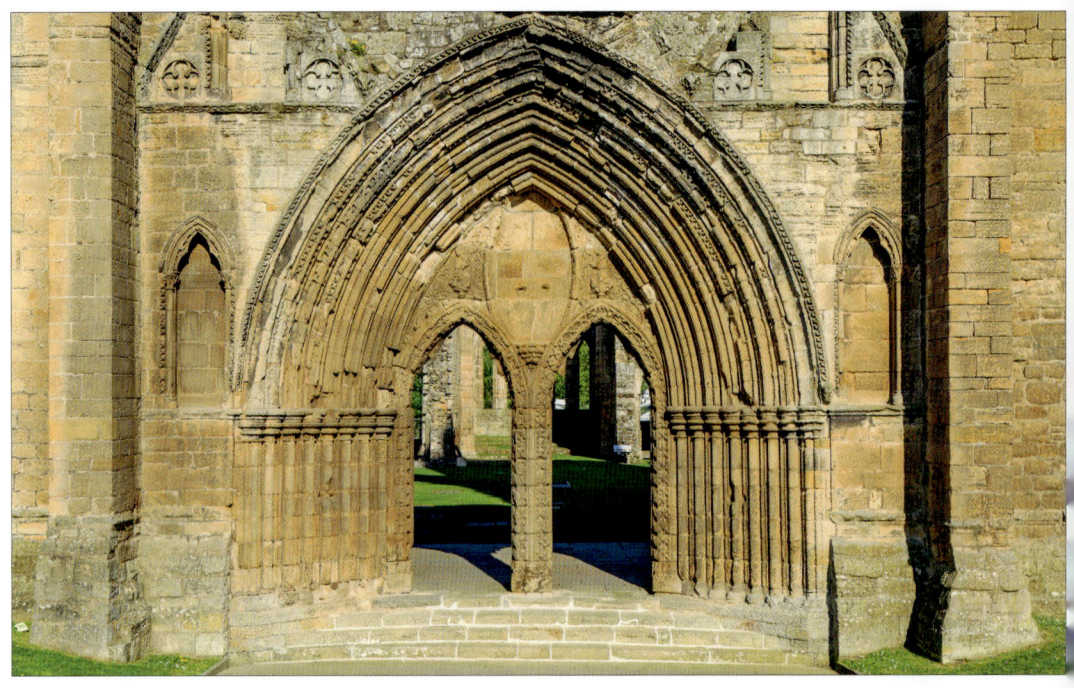

60 The great west doorway at the base of the towers was inserted after 1270. On each side, eight linked columns step diagonally inwards towards the doors, each with a finely carved arch rising from them.

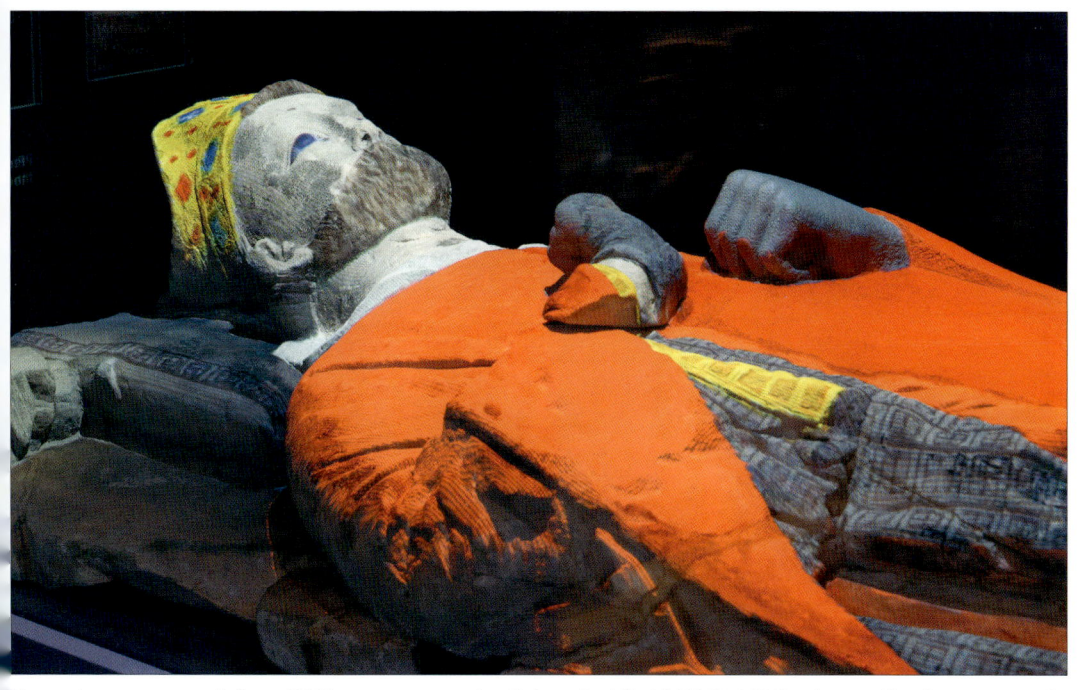

The enlargement work from 1270 was overseen by Bishop Archibald (1253-1298), whose effigy is displayed in the cathedral. At intervals, it is enlivened by the lighting effects shown above.

61

62 Looking down from the north-west tower gives a good idea of the cathedral's layout, from the crossing where the remains of the transepts can be seen on each side, through to the choir and presbytery.

The cathedral has a total length of about 85m/280ft following the 1270 enlargements.
Above: while up the tower, the view west over Cooper Park is not to be missed.

64 First built as part of the enlargement from 1270, the Chapter House of today is largely as rebuilt at the end of the 15th century. It is the only part of the cathedral that retains its roof.

Octagonal in shape, the fan vaulting is its finest feature. It provided a meeting place for the cathedral's clergy. These days it is also available for hire, generally as a wedding venue.

66 The cathedral precincts were surrounded by a large wall, with four defensible (i.e. with portcullis) gates ('ports'). Only Panns Port (the eastern one) remains, through which the cathedral can be seen.

A classic viewpoint for the east end of the cathedral is from across the River Lossie. This stretch of the river was notorious for flooding. Many restored carvings are on display at Elgin Cathedral . . .

68   ... the 'grotesques' in the upper pictures are decorative vault bosses. Lower left: this figure holds a bishop's crozier and a shield. Lower right: in medieval times, many tombs carried this skull-and-crossbones motif.

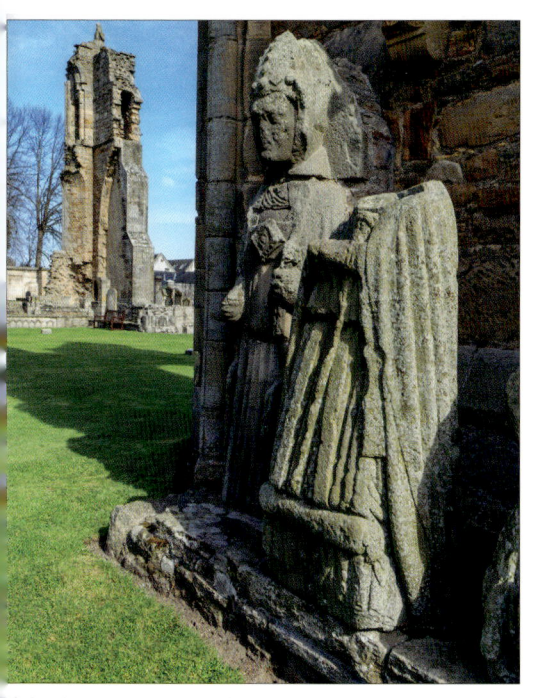

Left: the stone figure of a kneeling bishop that used to be high up on the central tower which collapsed in 1711. Right: the opposite side of the Pictish Stone pictured on p.6.

69

70 Across the road from the cathedral and often referred to as the Bishop's Palace, the Precentor's Manse has its crow-step gables accentuated by the snow. The Precentor was in charge of the Cathedral music.

This building is of national importance as a well-preserved example of a 16th-century manse belonging to one of the canons of Elgin Cathedral. Probably built about 1224, it reached its zenith when substantially . . .

72   . . . extended in 1557. This panorama takes in the east end of Cooper Park, the Precentor's Manse on the left, the Chapter House in the centre and the cathedral towers on the right. When built, these towers

(plus the former central tower) had spires as well. After the Reformation, decay and theft of materials took its toll, but what an amazing sight the cathedral must have been as built!

74 With a last and evocative view of the east end of the cathedral, a stone's throw away is Elgin's Biblical Garden (from where this picture was taken), situated just to the north of the cathedral.

This unique garden has 110 plants with biblical references. It opened to the public in 1996 and has been developed since then, for example by the addition of the Rock Garden from 2007 to 2011.

76 As well as growing the plants of the Bible, Bible stories are referenced by a number of statues. Here, for example, Jesus meets the Samaritan woman at the well (foreground); Samson is in the background.

Elgin's fortunes have always been affected by the River Lossie and its propensity to flood.
The new Landshut bridge by the cathedral is part of a recent £86million flood alleviation scheme.

78 Since 1797, Johnston's of Elgin has been making top quality cashmere and woollen garments and accessories. It also has an extensive homeware and gift range, sold from this building at its Elgin HQ.

This glorious autumn scene is in the garden at the back of the building pictured opposite. Inset: Cashmere goat sculpture at Johnston's. Tour complete, this is Elgin, from 'Castle to Cathedral to Cashmere'!

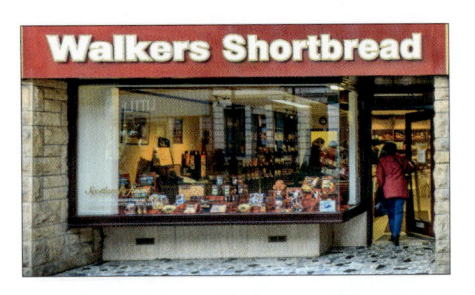

Published 2020 by Ness Publishing, 47 Academy Street, Elgin, Moray, IV30 1LR
Phone 01343 549663 www.nesspublishing.co.uk

All photographs © Colin and Eithne Nutt except front cover and pp 23 & 36 (left) © Ross Hunter; pp 2-3 & 5 © Lorraine Paterson; pp 4, 49 & 67 © Joanna Barnes; pp 12-13 © JP Photography; pp 36 (right) & 42 © Barry Whyte; p.43 (all) © Moray Motor Museum; pp 47 & 71 © Scott Innes; p.74 © Sheila Forbes

Printed in Malta

Text © Colin Nutt
ISBN 978-1-906549-85-5

All rights reserved. No part of this publication may be reproduced, stored in a retrieval system, in any form or by any means, without prior permission of Ness Publishing. The right of Colin Nutt as author of this work has been asserted by him in accordance with the Copyright, Designs and Patents Act 1988.

Front cover: Elgin Cathedral; p.1: carving of Elgin motto on the Muckle Cross; p.4: otter in Cooper Park; this page: Walkers Shortbread have traded in Elgin for over 50 years; back cover: Cooper Park

While Ness Publishing takes care to ensure all information is accurate, no responsibility can be taken for errors, or changes that occur after the book has gone to press.

Picturing Scotland books which most relate to the area around Elgin.

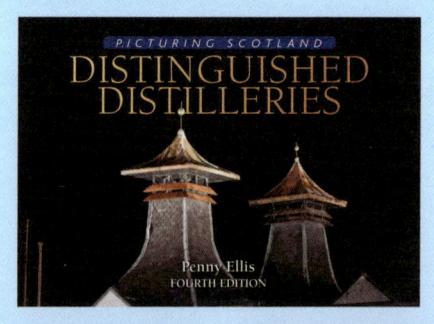

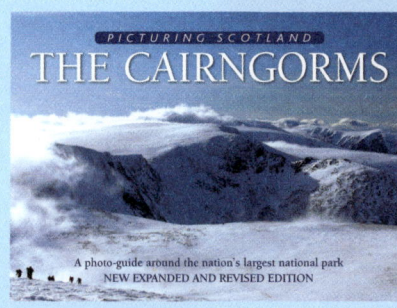

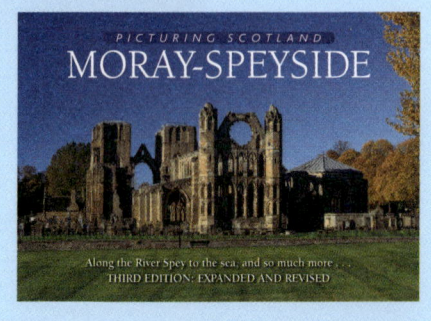